The Book
of
Cupcakes

Text by John Korduba

Drawings by Hanna Liu

ISBN: 979-8-39-613410-2

First printed edition 2023.

We who are about to diet
Salute you.

Acknowledgments

Project Manager **Peter Cerussi** nudged and nursed this book from gossamer idea to finished product. Graphic Designer **Angela Green** whipped the disparate files into a pleasing form. **Hanna Liu** provided illustrations that the accompanying texts can only hope to be worthy of. **Joanne Pagano Weber** submitted an Introduction that can stand on its own as a rapturous adventure in wordplay. And **Mindy Steinblatt** trained a gimlet eye on the whole manuscript, pointing out logical gaps. Any remaining errors are the fault of the author.

Also, a measure of gratitude must be offered to the counter people at the bakery department of my local supermarket. Over the course of two years, I would make a daily stop and buy a cupcake, thereby getting dubbed the "Cupcake Guy." On some days, after arriving late, the cupcake counters might be bare and I could be heard sighing, *"No cupcakes today?"* The response, *"Let me check in the back,"* would raise my hopes. And then a minute later, out might come an entire tray of cupcakes, or alternatively, a disappointed look with an instruction to come back tomorrow. In either case, this book is dedicated to them.

Introduction by Joanne Pagano Weber

The scent of vanilla wafts above the sidewalk and meanders to your nostrils, tempting you toward its source. Dear reader, are you a person who, in possession of a few dollars and in sight of a bakery window, simply cannot pass it by? And might you, like me, I sheepishly admit, be even less inclined to do so if, in that window, cupcakes are prominently displayed?

You think, I'll just look, I must get to work, I'll have to put in an extra thirty minutes on the treadmill, I'm getting closer, I'll keep going, I won't look. But. You step inside and delirious confusion overtakes you. Which one shall you choose? Three, of course. And you think, am I the only person like this? There must be a study or something.

Comrade of the perennial sweet tooth, look no further. In *The Book of Cupcakes*, author John Korduba has given us a sympathetic and conspiratorial nod. On these pages you find the delectable wisdom of children, whimsical kitchen economics, imaginative history, and the confectionary foibles of humankind from the seven decadent peccadilloes to the odd twists and turns of love. Proving once again that cupcake philosophy can be Biblical in scope.

The Book of Cupcakes, preciously illustrated by Hanna Liu, celebrates your sugary delight in ways that you will recognize with a smile. Prepare to savor your favorite dessert in its company and find yourself on its pages. Absolve yourself from guilty indulgences past as you take another bite. You will feel vindicated for every lecture meted out by well-meaning, calorie-counting friends and relatives who are blind to the heaven of devouring the cake in the cup.

More than this, John Korduba, poet/philosopher, journalist, video-maker, and writer of *Everybody Gets Lost in Brooklyn*, gives us something that we are all yearning for. A moment in our fraught and technologically driven times to pause, hold a book of joy in our hands, chuckle, and be kind to ourselves. In a world of so little sweetness, that is a gift indeed.

In the beginning ...was the cupcake.

(My personal Creation myth.)

An apple per day may keep the
doctor away.

But a cupcake at night,
brings to the darkness,
some light.

"It's too sweet," she says,
pushing the cupcake away.

"But how can anything be too
sweet?" he asks,

whistling through his teeth.

If a cupcake is cut in half
Is it now two?

Yes, of course!

One for me
and
One for me, too.

"You can't have your [cup] cake
and eat it too."

Whoever said this never lived
near a bakery.

So many cupcakes,
so little stomach.

"Let them eat cake," a queen
once said,

and soon thereafter lost her
head.

But, you know, I'm thinking,
maybe if

she'd offered instead, a cake in
a cup,

the royal head might still be
up.

Experts have been debating
whether it is more proper to
eat a cupcake with a fork or a spoon.

Myself, I prefer eating with a
spoon, but keeping

the fork handy in case needed
to fight off demanding
neighbors.

Vanilla cupcake or chocolate?
It's a tough decision.
But if you eat either one
then it's a simple choice
to also eat the other.

How many sprinkles can fit on
the head of a cupcake?

While you're rubbing your
eyes and considering this, I
will steal your cupcake.

(I was never good at math, but
I know how to take one from one.)

Classic

Mini

Cutie

The problem with
having a cupcake
for breakfast
is that the
rest of the day
can't possibly
measure up.

One cupcake...
two cupcakes...
three cupcakes...

Hmm...
what comes after three?

(Widening the belt –
probably.)

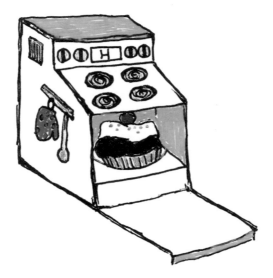

Where to go in the afterlife for
a good cupcake?

I'm guessing Heaven got the
nicer bakers,

but probably

Hell has the better ovens.

Feeling stressed today.
(No cupcake is safe.)

The waitress approaches,
bearing a tray with a birthday
cupcake.

Its lit candle brightens your
face, as everyone sings.

And later - best part - when
they begin

dividing the check,
you owe only a thank you.

To whomever took my
cupcake from the office fridge
yesterday,

just to tell you that I'm also
missing a thumb tack,

for which you might check
your seat cushion.

Cupcake, how do I love thee?
Let me count the whey(s).

Some people arc quite firm in resisting a tempting cupcake.

Myself, being of weaker stock, when offered what I should not have,

I hear a devilish voice saying, "Don't fight the filling."

A quiet restaurant
A small table
One cupcake with two forks
A young couple
One face serious,
the other happy, unsuspecting
Words are exchanged
A moment later
the waiter removes one of the
forks.

Should a cupcake be eaten
starting from the left or starting
from the right?

Says one, "From the left, of
course, for we know best how the
rest should go."

Says the other, "From the right,
of course,
and we won't follow their
guidance -oh, no."

But perhaps if both together dug
in, t'would solve the riddle,
when both mouths meet in the
middle.

It is not known when the first
cupcake was created.

However
it is believed

that it coincided with the first
hearing of the "Mmmm"
sound.

The ancient lawgiver
Hammurabi once said,

"An eye for an eye
And a tooth for a tooth."

Fair enough! Say I.

But if you eye your
neighbor's cupcake with the
thought of sinking a tooth
into it,

you may end up gaining the
cupcake at the cost of losing
the tooth, my friend.

This morning, I am eating a cupcake.

Of course, only a small one because I am super-disciplined! Just like the ancient Romans, those world conquerors, who brought many provinces

-for example, Mauritania-

under their sway.

Hmm...(As I pour some coffee.)

You know, I'm thinking, a larger cupcake might be okay. And I'll run the risk if Mauritania slips away.

The difference between Daylight
Savings time and Standard time
is that

in the first one

you can start eating your cupcake
an hour earlier

while in the other

you can't actually remember
eating the cupcake

but you know it's gone.

I'd like to thank the
Cupcake Writers Hall of Fame

for giving me this prestigious
award.

It's the nicest thing to happen to
me since breakfast.

And,
in the end, the cupcake
you take

is equal to the cupcake
you bake.

Contributors

Peter Cerussi

is a PMP certified project manager with experience at a global law firm. He now devotes much of his time to creative pursuits, such as posting funny videos on YouTube. This is his first book project. Reach out to Peter at pctoner@hotmail.com.

Angela Green

has been a graphic designer for 20 years. In addition to this book, she also designed John Korduba's previous book. She can be reached at angelakgreen@gmail.com.

John Korduba

is the author of *Everybody Gets Lost in Brooklyn*. Follow him on Instagram at BrooklynBoi_2019.

Hanna Liu

is a passionate High School teacher in Taiwan who tries to bring happiness to the people around her. She is reachable via hanna5201114@hotmail.com.

Joanne Pagano Weber

is an artist and writer who exhibits in the tri-state area. She has created the sets for the Hudson Valley New Year's Day Spoken Word/Performance Extravaganza since 2020. She is co-curator of Dialogues for the Ear and Eye, a cross-disciplinary salon for the arts. Email Joanne at joey3girl@gmail.com or find her on Instagram at joannepaganoweber.

Made in the USA
Columbia, SC
08 November 2023

25485314R00035